PREGNANCY OF THE EARTH

Pregnancy of the Earth

A collection of poems
by

DONNY BARILLA

BOOKS

Adelaide Books
New York / Lisbon
2020

PREGNANCY OF THE EARTH
A collection of poems
By Donny Barilla

Published by Adelaide Books, New York / Lisbon
adelaidebooks.org

Editor-in-Chief
Stevan V. Nikolic

For any information, please address Adelaide Books
at info@adelaidebooks.org
or write to:
Adelaide Books
244 Fifth Ave. Suite D27
New York, NY, 10001

ISBN: 978-1-953510-20-4

Printed in the United States of America

Sierra, thank you for the friendship

Contents

I humbly quiver to the seeds of the earth.

Carved Creek

Since several rotations around the sun, in moments
the creek carved into the woodlands and through the narrow
slice of the meadow which humbled along the breath
of the trembling dash of the sulking sky.

Upon drinking until I gently filled with the clearest
moans of the sweetwater, severing by the honey hive and sap
of the maple.

The fog descended and walked across the fields, alive as phantoms
which soothed and patterned across me.

Gently, I felt the pulse of the droplets of dew which softened
each grass blade and clever patch of weed.

I return to the fumbling creek and moaned into the wind
as rivets and dancing rapids swept across me and tucked
beneath my burrowing flesh, sweetly caressed by the rising sun.

Passage

From the hollows of the woods, I pass and hear the trembling
voice of every ache of the phantom which sauntered to the passage
dwelling by feet and by ankle and calf.

I soothe my way through the floods of every wind.
softly, I lay beneath a scattering of trees and I relish
in the drip of each mineral as each pouch of soil
welcomes the enhancement of the empty voice.

I search the path which leads me to the echo of resonance,
the curve of the stream.

With a blaze of this search, this moan of the stream,
I stop, drink and fasten to the ghost of her as once
she stood naked before me and I paused my palm
across the fullness of her breasts.

I walk this endless path into the groomed, rich earth.

Opened Blouse

The sky opened as a blouse and with the tremble of her breasts,
the dash of the creams and rains which flooded the earth
loosened upon me and I fell to the sweet
dance of every curling leaf.

Most gentle, I covered your lulling gifts.

The press of my feet deepened into the
spread of every flicker of soil,
and reach of the depress of branch and fallen vine,
I stood upon the vapors where you sweetly left me;
I slipped to the grasses beneath my feet
and found you moist and alive.

I the last of moments, I look upon you and the fade of you
Tenderly, the haze and the flickering mist.

Apricots and Pinks

The oak roots deepened as fangs well into the soil and the treasures
of every throb an thirst.

Heavy hour of night, spread as velvet across the cloak of the sky,
I settled upon the softness of the moss of the breadth of the tree.

I tumble upon the the stretch of the trunk and quickly, the leaves
caress me in scents of an earlier season and I surrender.

In the final moment of night, the sky shatters
into apricots and pale pinks.
I settle upon each morning ribbon and I burrow at last.

Lingering Smoke

Across the fields, I edged my way to the base of the sloping
gown of this wooded hill, I spoke of you with every patch.

Soil groomed in moisture and coddled each slumbering tree,
by Autumn, I stayed and watched the leaves caress.

I found her in the in the grotto of wavering ferns.
I rested upon her until I loosened into the earth.

The fog spread across us and lingered as smoke.

Rising to the summit of the peak of these trembling hills,
I entered you with all moaning soil and sweet majestics.

Finality of the Soil Where I Rest

The caverns tossed echoes across the mountainside
which sauntered and trembled as a dance.

I paused by the glistening floods which
soothed through the deepest edge
of the valley and spread through every meadow.

Upon this reach, I suckled every trim of every spoken
word which I bathed upon and listened to.

Reaching to the deepest of caverns, I rest, sleep hear in slouching
rhythms which dampen me to the finality of this soil.

Waiting for Fog

The open womb of the tender, rich soil of the valley tugged forth
in moisture and settled through spread of the onion root and
rise of the thicket which suckled upon the
tense edge where drifting leaves
spooled upon the thorns and trellised upon the passing waters.

Now, in the fullness of the falling rains, I
walked the edge of the earth
then crossed the fracture where the soils
moaned having spirited waters slash
every root, branch and crimping leaf.

In the end of day, the flicker of light, I follow the ghost of her
endless into the sweet grasses of the breadth of her as the step
of each foot rose from the fog, the most distant of mountains.

We Return to the Earth

Upon this endless walk, I blend with
the tans and reds of the forest
which claims me.

I open my mouth and gently, I breath every
breath as I loosen to the ponds,
wade soft through every stream; I release
the fog of the rich soil of the floor,
bed of the earth.

You spread through the woodlands of the trembling earth.

I follow you as the vapors of Autumn and
sweetly I carve the flesh of you
along the deep of the thrashing stream.

I fade into the spices you caress with as
each grip of the wildflower;
together, we groom as the slithering fog of the gentle earth.

Pilgrimage to the Deep of the Forest

Into the woodlands, I pouch and pause as the mask of the earth.

I swoon the thin creek which fastens each slight of flickering sun,
trapped and hurried each leaf
wavers as the light burrows with speed.

I open myself to the green vest of the earth;
Quiet and motionless, the mesh of the approaching gnashing
Fangs of Winter roamed robustly and silent.

The evening gown of the Winter sky, cloaked the dance
Of the forest bed which stiffened as the freeze of the maple.

With the schedule of the visions of her upon the white snowbed
She lay in the quivering dark as I look and loosen her from
The wedge of the forest deep.

Leaving You I Favor the East

The bedsheets rested as an ocean cove, filled
with warmth and moisture.

I reached her upon the ledge of sand and pebbles which crooned
every fleeting beat of the brine and pasture
where I fastened and filed each
corner of the fullness of the bed with cream of the drizzling tide.

With my lips upon the full shadow of your breast, I suckled every
sting of the whipping lash of the sky.

She approached me with salted, drizzling
water as the breads of her
caressed and flooded me in the tremble
of the earliest clip of morning.

Leaving the bedroom, I fastened my
denim and cottons as the wind
directed me east so I roamed the soils of the earth;
the waxing of the flashes threaded me in rivets and sauce.

Flesh and the Seed of Her Womb

I host the verb of the earth, tangled with
glances of the flawless sun.
She replied with the warmest floods of
air, threading across the meadow
which deepened with every step.

I gave her the child of each passing elm tree
which freshened with each groan
of the glazed pearl beads of morning and the leaves which fall
quietly upon the suckling steps at nightfall.

Into the grove of the fullest apples, I snapped
into this flesh and thought
of each powder upon you skin: breast,
clavicle, abdomen, thigh and groin.

She came to me in the boldness of naked sky.
With the glaze of this sweet meadow, I
coddled each seed of her sweet womb.

I Search for Her In the High Grass

I swam through the gestures of the breathing high grasses
which leaned to the slant of the warming Spring sun.

She placed her palm upon the pouch of my groin and lulled
me to the perfect basket coating the
earth as I loosened her blouse
and kissed her pale, full breast.

By the last nightfall of the spread of
Autumn, I awoke to the lounging
of these gathering leaves which crinkled
and sweetly faded upon the dusts of the gripping wind.

She roamed eagerly through the fallen
seed and the dew which dashed
upon the grass blade and I tremble to the touch
of the spices of sweet flesh which relished in the lounging floods,
sulking to the advance of tenderness.

I await the touch of her sweet lips
into the tenderness which soaks upon me;
she dances through the lusty breath
of the sweet dance of the perfect meadow and cream.

Awaiting Winter

Bold Winter winds slice through the
empty mountainside and slash
open each ancient branch which freezed
upon the fleece of heavy ice.

Every white bed of snow fluttered a pass of Wintery dusts.

I searched for my reunion with the lime colored growth of buds
and pods which loosen to the melding grass and fading snow.

The mountainside begged for the wealth of green sweet blossoms
upon the tender bloods of the sap of the trees.

I hike my way to the mountain peak and
I settle and wait for the swell
of the pregnancy of the tender coat of the soil of the earth.

Nocturnal Spices

I carved my way through the apricot
and placed my fingers across
the breads of your abdomen and gently, I
kissed you in all your paleness.

Your thighs spoke as an open field.
I breathed your tender wheats which wavered by the richest soil

I opened your lips and threaded so
sweetly; I fastened to the crimp
of your flooding gales. I listened to the hearth
of this towering oak tree and the swell of each pasture.

Morning sun shatters through the bay
window and I hold these particles of scent and spice.

Pearled Dew Drops

Upon bathing in the silver moonlight, I rested
by the pond and trembled with her dancing wrists and fingertips.

I listened and the pines slashed into the gushing breeze.

Into the floods of the sudden dash of rainfall, I
spoke sweetly with the opened blouse and gathered her
breasts to the beads which trembled like the pearl
which dampened through each stretch of cotton.

The pond gently grew still at the moment before morning.
lastly, a flicker of the moon, then raced to the swiftness
of the rise of the grip of the sun.

Waiting for Rain

I walked across the tan burns of the grass which crunched
to the spread of my feet and boot.

Soothing upon the gestures of each mineral of the coarseness
of the soil, I bloomed to the perching sweat
of my chest, back and forehead.

In a dash of the cooler lulling and the pause of each second,
I motioned to the rise of the breeze which tempts me in floods
where the softness of the night, I trembled eagerly.

Well into the moment of midnight, I felt the crimping soil
fasten and swell with tapping rain.

The boldness of quiet sauces relish into
the death and burden of each
brown blade, I surrender to the passage of tender moonlight.

Dazzling Sun

I suckled from the tremble of her breast.
Dazzling showers of sun caressed each pause as I reached
and swiftly found you.

I lost my way so sweetly into the lamplight of the Summer gleam
upon frequenting you, I soothe my mouth upon your summit.

I fell to the slick pastures of the robee upon your abdomen,
the garden cove of the sweet cavern, I swelled upon you.

The prism of her eyes slung in patterns where sulking moistures
of her mouth dances upon me.

Dancing Branches

Sinking to the threshold of the woodland
path, charms and sweet gestures
rise and swell into the sliver of her womb.

I reach my hand to the pebble suckling on the dirt and clays
which rest as a burden upon each gathered crust.

Mosses and lulls of the ferns spend every
moment of homage as fractured
fittings open to the quaking spread; sweetly I loosen upon you.

Reaching the sulk of the valley, I witness the
pour where each rivet of the creek
moistens the earth and I reach to you in heavy glazes.

I slept in the vast clutter of the dancing
and motioning forest deep.

Crossing the Edge of Morning

The new moon slept and sauntered with the black
cloak which reach across in the darkest of clouds.

She moaned with the patterns of my cool, trembling fingers.
I edged into the breads of her as the whispers of these powdered
pouches I suckled, quivered in the spread of this heavy nightfall.

I spoke in the fury of temptation.

I walk the endless shoreline as the sauces of this
pink and purple ribboned sky ordained
me to the depth of the earth.

Return

Shallow curves of the tender river spoke to the driftwood.
I wade in all nakedness as the pebbles upheld me in the depth
of the channel and rapids.

Sweet scents drifted through the currents and sank with the glaze
of each fallen leaf.

Alone, I pictured you, here last Spring, and
I caressed you in the fullness
of your shadowed breasts and the quiver of
each lip and each roaming arm.

The draft swept upon me.
I reach the edge of the northern bank which sulked upon me as I
coddled my way to the denims and cottons
of the fury of this blended river.

Pregnancy of the Earth

I covet the seed of the earth as tossed
and burrowing hands deepen
through the minerals and the soil which
moans sweetly across me.

Near, the oak fractures and splinters to
the verbs of the tangling egg
as sweet rains moisten and luster forth.

I speak to the galaxies which tremble and
scatter with the fertile robes
and garments, quietly each thread croons
for the muds of paternal
flickering jousts of a rendezvous with sweet motion.

Coming in the vests of the fields and meadows, I place my palms
upon the earth as saps of the maple tree
lathers my crackling woods.

Tenderly, we saturate and swim across
the breadth of the swift river.

I drink each bead of the water of the heavy earth.

Belly of the Lake

Into the blitz of the crumbling sky, I kneel upon the saddle
of the burrowing sweet fields, so secretly alive.

The dance of the warmth of each flickering dash of wind
tangles through the tamp as my boots
deepen upon the soil of the earth.

Summer verbs thrash with the fullness
of every leaf against every leaf.
I soothe as the polish of the falling rains in the dome of the sky.

Watching the growth of the belly of the swelling lake, I
moan into the passions of the groin and slowly,
the womb drinks each droplet of rain and
fulfills in creams and sweet butters
as the climate of the cavern suckles this domain.

Path Into the Blossoming Womb

I taste the sweat of the moist earth
sweetly and tenderly upon the edge of my tongue.

I spoke to you and the lather of the pale, flickering thighs
crooned and swooned with the dance of the river,
the dance of the creek and flex of the ocean's tides.

Each bead of each trembling translucent pearl
paused upon the swelling glimpse of her breasts.

I paused my lips to the fastened saps as the breath of these winds
rattled into the wealth of this sweet union of earth and the cascade
of the majesty of the sky.

Caressing you with the smoothness of my hands,
I croon my path into the stretch of your blossoming womb.

Quivering Glades

As I spoke to the threads of the gathered mints, aromas slithered well
into my lungs and filled me.

Gently, these calloused hands stamped
the breads of this moist earth; I
dug and loosened the soil which lent
softly the enigma and I stood
to the quivering glades.

Endlessness roamed upon the sweep of the lofting dusts.
I tremble upon the sweet gestures of the
dancing buds and silent pods
which burst in surrender as temper of the earth and glazing fumes
sulk and moan to the heaviest meadow.

By nightfall, I feel the pulse of these saplings and breasts.

In the most fertile fields of clover, shoots and the onion sprout,
I lush to the quiver of the vine and spread of your nakedness,
leaves trace across you and I burrow my path upon you.

Travelling North

Your breath spread warmth across the
motions and tremble of this meadow,
so alive in the floods of the morning fog and evening mist.

Hurriedly, I reach the fastened end and look to the north.
I watch the white beds as each leans upon
the mountain and the sloping curve
of every rocky cliff molds to the sauce
of the valley and the meadow
of the valley.

Lost in the whimper of the loosened birth
of the wildflower and green buds
sloping to the tender summit,
I rested and slept into the graves of the earth.

Past the dampness of the morning glen,

Sweat shatters across the blade of grass as the peak

Of midday carves me in moans, seed and bud.

Evening Visit

You gather me from the threads of the blanket,
Wools which gingerly soften me in particles
Of touch.

The rhythms of each soothing
voice as you bend wildly through the room,
I sweeten my hands upon you as each echo floods across me.

Your fingers, trembling as ice,
You fasten to me in thirst as this parchment voice
Drinks from the pouch of these creamed, quivering breast.

You lather as the foamed cove of the ocean,
Sweet gems of the pearl and ancient fossil,
I stand so close as the salted kelp angles across my flesh.

Looking to the wavering perch of the room,
The candle shakes shadows and gently
I call upon the quiver of your lips.

Late Visit

There rested breasts upon my cheek and
fastened to the down pillows.
I spoke to her of the eager paleness of her womb
as floods of this pulse and creams of her
full flesh suckled with retort.

I stretched my hands across hamstrings and thighs.
the clamor of the woodlands, reaching
beyond the stretch of the patio,
swiftly tempted me to the deepened dark
realm of the cedar chipped path.

With your nakedness and with my nakedness, I
swim gently through the stream, edge to edge.

I awaken and flinch to the tremble of morning light.
you vanish to the writhing shrubs and
fade into the gnarled thicket
which creeps endlessly upon the wooded earth.

Escaping the Warmth

I roast soothingly beneath the press of the sun.
Tenderly, the red maple cast shadows of the branches
And so sweetly I watch the haze and the dust as the evening
Opens as a grave.

Burgundy leaves flood the pasture
as every crimping vein and curled cup caves into the dust;
I rest beneath the trunk and suckle the soft breeze.

The miles rode fast beneath me as the
woodlands soon approached.
So near the wooded edge, I looked upon
a murder as the low clouds
Flecked and danced in peppers throughout the sky.

I ached into the endless shadow as the trembling spread of time
And fallen dust whispers in grooves of the
water springs, trickling as a dance.

Each tree bud boasted of these woods
as a eager shade and shadow
Upon the leafy floor spoke of seeds and the snap of the bud.

From the North

I open myself to the vest, mosses and ferns, a
calm spread upon the pasture
of the quiet meadow which trembles
to the sweet breeze threading
across the vast hills far to the north.

Resting patiently to the milkweed and the onion grass,
I lurk so close to the honey hive.

I feel the swift dance of the emerald grass
which reaches and grooms
upon my boots.

The soothing crimp where the pinecones,
chipped and fractured, loosen, I
hear the crunch and moan as every needled quilt lays beneath me.

Gently, off the edge of my face and neck, I
feel the fullness of the breath
of this gesture which blooms across the towering climb.

Refuge in the Woodlands

I glance to the blue sweeping sky with
humble spreads of cotton threaded
clouds masking the silent sun.

As I wait into the deep of evening, I feel
the touch of sweet wildflowers
trembling into the fallen cloak of the darkest velvet.

So swiftly, I enter the shadow of these woods
which swoon over me, lulling
in silence.

Each grave of every spread where the seed blossoms,
I find the newest growth of tender life, as
once burrowed into the mulch, soil
and cedar chips hosting as a benediction.

I speak of the madness of the dark of the woodlands.
Softly, I tremble into the blush and breath
as silence gushes across me.

Past Midnight in Blankets and Quilts

Sweetly, I lay in patterns upon every
blanket and the softest of quilts.
the gently theshing winds tap and swoon against the window
which grooms the edge of the eager house.

Amidst the middle of this trembling house, I touch the softness
of you and sweeten the milk of your full breasts.

This instrument of quivering nightfall blossoms into every stitch
as the seed of the earth melds upon the deep of the earth.

I peak to the carry of the wind.

Gentle bloom and blossom of the groin, thickened into the thick
soils beneath, I carry the heavy aromas to
the deep of your quivering lips.

Upon This Bedding

Through thicket and thorn, I burrow into
the majesty of the dampness
of the woods which broom swiftly upon me.

I reach the bedding of the pause here upon
needles and leaves, pinecones
and acorns as silently I lay and slumber.

I sweeten my path as the cold rains flash quickly upon me.

Moments past Winter I return to the grip of the earth.

Resting Shell

I look to the eastern peach hues of the
morning flank of the morning rise.
I hear the moans of the endless rapture,
waves caressing the shoreline.

Sweetly, the sun crawls from the horizon and
glimpses in the slowest motions.

The shell as resting upon the sand, so many thousands
of leagues and rotations across the humble
sun, I turn and walk the shadow
Which glimpses to the earth.

I reflect upon the nocturnal bloom of the
my previous encounter with
every shadow of night.

I speak to the trembling lush of each curve
as slowly, I approach the deep
of the smash of this slithering brine.

Into the Flesh of Morning

With pause and patient recollection,
I drew the cream of the sweetest breasts as quietly you lulled
me into the tender dream of the tender earth.

I slept upon you as each breath heaved and spread across me.

Well into the first moment of morning, I felt the sweet grass
tamp beneath the press of my feet. The
pink fires of the eastern sky
trickled and fell upon me.

I knelt and drank from the freshest of trickling mountain streams.

Moss slipped over the slick reach of the heaviest of stones
as the leaves gathered across each trembling, passing wind.

The occasional quiver of each dance of each dark shadowed green,
spoke to me in gestures of the breads of
the woodland and iced water
which fed the soils of every nook of the forest.

As She Fades in Vapors

With trembling skies, I spoke softly to the grooming meadow.
I look to the slope of the spreads of grass and swiftly, I lulled
my breath upon her as quiet iced fingers and delicate palms
opened her before me.

The smashing rains and darkness of the deep rose
as the press of my groin rose to the powders of her gentle flesh.

Quietly, I looked to the woods and watched her walk across
the fields as a fade of the fullest vapors.

I walked an endless path as quietly, I feel
the earth soften beneath me.

In the Open Meadow

The hues of your walnut colored hair loosens,
softly floods in the breath of every open meadow.

From your naked flesh, I smell the fragrances of each
posture and glance, the full wind opens as the gestures of each
touch stirs you upon me.

In the smash of the fullness of the breeze I feel you quiver
sweetly in the cool palms of my hands.

This night will approach as a fever and groom
into the sweat of Summer nocturnes.

In the end, I walk the meadows and blaze across the trembling
dance of every silence which grooms me
in the groin of the approach
of the cove where I recall your delicate touch.

Youthfulness

Walking to South Mountain, I took into my lungs
every scent of every leaf which remained
slicked beneath my boots
as the evening rained in trembling coolness.

The oak reached upon the wind
as every branch thrust and wavered across the swift winds.

We met beneath the deep cover of the dense moaning trees.
I touched her and drove her to nakedness.

By the edge of morning light, we rest
upon the moss covered stones
and spoke well into the lowering fog which moaned across us.

I look back upon the swift age of my recall of soothing youth.
resting by the oak, I hear the scurry of the dancing wind.

Together in the Woods

She placed her warm hands upon my neck and soothingly
spoke vowels as the candle flickered from
the slightly opened window.

My thin lips paused upon her breasts as
she dressed the moon in velvets
and gently spread the nights sky across
the hot posture of our flesh.

The flooding enhancement of the sweet
majestic stretch of the glen,
drew the sauces of the earth and I snatched every pinecone
and chipped wooden nut; the soil tossed every scent.

Hearing the soothing wind as each gush
tapped upon this home with
each corner of each wall, looked to the deep
of the woodlands, we smelled the sweet
marrow of the gentle earth.

End at the Mountain Peak

Walking tenderly upon the white beds, gown of the meadow,
so soft in the departure of the earth, I
stood for a moment and watched
the remaining leaves fall upon the patch of the fleece, the end
of the scattered dust in the darkest tans.

The trail led me to the northern peak
which opened as a loosening
of a cotton shirt; white snow carved each way across the supple
valley and the rise of the near mountain peak.

In the next moment, I watched her descend as the swooning
enticement of the sulking fog which sweetly caressed the soil,
tree branch and freeze of the rocks, crossed across the deep
of the valley's trembling stream.

I hear the moan of the lashing winds as
I gently fall to the icy ground.

Burial by the Stream

The night spoke to me as the wash of the stream spread
to the edges of the curve of the slithering rapids.

I awoke to this and walked to the trembling sounds;
the piles and mounds of leaves chanted beneath me; the
pooling eddies of the sweet water hushed me in silence
as tender blooming dances of the breeze echoed across me.

Now, I leaned upon the tremor of the open dome of the sky.

I leaned to the sweet of the red maple tree.
In the dash of a moment, I slept within
the cakes and muds of the earth.

Longest Hike

Resting upon the saddle of the fallen birchwood
from the deeply carved spread of this dying woods,
I sat and soft winds caressed my face and full hair;
I surrender to the slumbering woods
and spoke gently of the burial,
the benediction of the mourning press of grooming mist.

I gather my things and my walking stick as I roam endless
into the vast flooding breath of this woodland voice,
fallen leaves and the snap of the twig.

Midday Sun

He spoke to the deepest caverns which rest tender and silent.
I watch him as he hovers across the shattering pinks of morning;
an endless pouch of the heaviest waters, He sweetly touches
the basin and mountain of the ocean, carved in tender eons,
I wait for the call which saunters near me as a ghost.

Eons past, I swoon through the patterns of each tremble
from which I caress the lips of her.
by the instance of nightfall I awake and shed myself of every robe
and cloth and I wade soft into the foam
and kelp of the morning sea.

Peeking to the midday sun, I mian and lose my way.

I Smell Night's Fragrance

I reach beneath these silk robes and I discover the creams of life.

In a moment's touch, I listen to her fumbling mouth quiver
upon the dance of the down bed.

Softly, I spoke upon the frailty of her pale powdered ears
and I touch the pale powders of her moist
groin which reveals me in the rise
of the waning fog.

The candle spoke to the calm voices of the room as I
shared the beads of sweat as she tenderly lay before me.

By morning, the candle had tossed all flicker and wax
as I listened to her warm breath;
the sun captured the dusts as they
lofted through the bed, carpet and her soft caress.

Waiting for Spring

You spoke to me of the empty woods
which held the moon as a candle,
soft and distant in the sky.

We walk this narrow path as humid fumes
left our mouth and I found
a gathering of branches which fell to this
burial in the fracture of night.

I paused and kissed her, so gently
I heard the moans of the empty womb of the earth.

Dampness of the carve of the patches
of snow which glazed tenderly
across the floor of the forest and rock laden path,

You ran the touch of your hand against the
softness of my neck and shoulder.

I felt the bones upon the icy earth and
freed the marrow into my breath.

Treasures and charms of the frozen bud spoke to the raspy wind.

On the zenith of Spring, I loosened you
upon the moss and shadowed ferns.

Fields of Eager Wheat

Upon the dredge of Spring, the aromas
fill me, then collapse within me.
I feel the threads of every stitch and hem
soak the press of the sweats born of bead
as each tugs upon the cottons
of my shirt and trembles across my back.

I pause, sit upon the patio and sipped the chestnut colored coffee.

I sink into the climate and open my lips
as the winds surface and hold me
in the treasury of Spring warmth which
feeds upon the slick sweat
of my flesh, I watch the budding tree
limbs and walk to the spread,
the glaze upon the sweet meadow and fields of eager wheat.

Evening's End

Early morning, I fasten my eyes to the tangerine sky;
sweet waves caress across the heavy ocean's gleam.

The winds from a further east groom me in threads
of the salted brine.

I spoke gently to the wash of the sea cove birds which tuck
beneath the crest of rippling foam.

The lavish flicker of each instance of approaching moonlight,
I grow tender as the wilt of my skin soaks the dripping sun
and soothes to the pause of daylight.

I lean my face to the west and welcome the treasure of night.

Walk in the Countryside

The breath of the mouth of the sky, opened as a gale
Sweeping and washing across me.

Reaching grasses licked upon my ankles and calves,
The rise of the onion weed spoke to me of hunger and thirst.

Looking above the edge of the orange marmalade sky,
My sight flickered with the trembling wind.

I sipped the blistering fumes and chestnut hues
Of the coffee and sweetly, the fog clamored across the soft earth.

After a gentle pause, I walk into the quiet
garden of the grotto and glen.

Tales

The wicker cover and shave of the birchwood whispered of tales
of the recent collapse of Winter.

The resounding crunch of the packed
snow, tight as a layer of foam,
sulked with the deepened step of the tamp of my boots.

Clouds fell and suckled as smoke which
clung to the soft melt of the earth.

I came upon a slender, empty wood.
crows swaggered across the treetops as the coldest of wind
fluttered and flickered each wing.

Stopped, I clung to the grip of the packed stretch of icy snow.
a branch snapped with the current which
tossed through the opened breeze.

Swiftly the sky faded to pepper as the dusty
snow tumbled across distant fields.

By the Buds in April

Standing upon the center on a slight jettison peak,
I remain straight with shoulders crest and
collected the wrapping cool
air across every edge of my face.

Paused, then the winds scurried back in gales and whips which
tore through every cloth and burned in ices across my flesh.

I listened to her as she spoke of rebuttal and retort,
she spoke of the circling of the earth
and the circling of the moon.

Well upon the hazed madness of the
burials of the fullest bloom of
January, I deepened across a glaze of ice.

By April I quivered with the shaking buds of morning which
wrapped across my taste of clover and the wildflower.

I look beyond my shoulder and faced to the west.
the wheat fields bloomed to the dancing
crypt of tangled daylight.

Ocean Deep

Resting upon the dunes of sand which fumbled across the stretch
of the shoreline,
I lathered in every slip of foam and suckle of kelp.

I listened keenly and heard her speak
with the tongues of the licking
water crest as the cool winds slapped

Every pinch of ancient grains and ancient nook of the shell.

I felt the moisture of my burgundy flesh
as the slither of the brine
caressed my tensed leathery shell.

I spoke to the breath which carried upon the sweet winds
and I received the aromas of the Autumnal arrival.

I slipped my way into the breads
of the earth and craved and carved my way to hunger
which spread my rib upon the ocean deep.

I look upon the rooftops of the trees,

Sweetly, buds snap open and sink in dark, rich soils.

Dusts on the Skyline

Hanging fangs, the loose branch of the willow tree
touched, draped the Autumn leaves of
the canvas of this soil and rock.

Resting against the smoothest of trunks, I felt the threads
of my denim groove on moss and tumbling
slivers of crimped leaves.

Swift, trembling gasps of the warmest air flickered across
every cool edge of my face and wind slap my burning neck.

A few seconds before nightfall, I fade upon the dusts of the field,
clinging to the gasp of the blooming skyline.

Shedding my path across the grass, tucked in this meadow,
I shelter by the roots and dance to the
floundering breath where each
groove of each seed grooves.

Thanos

The carpet of the Summer woods, held
fabrics of mulch and chips of wood.
upon the farthest reach of ferns and moss and tangled greens,
I lay in a soft quiver and slept gently as
visions of the wrapping vine;
silently, I fall to the touch of tan and orange piles of leaves.

The voices of the patient wait for the ferry to cross the thick
of the river, edging sweetly.

A swollen tender leaf from the snap of the red maple drifts
sequentially across the deep of these kelp filled waters.

In the life of the youth, I fade to the reach of the trembling fist.

Sif

Locks upon the ocean wind, flaxen hue.
I caress and soften the heaviest of
hammers, thick upon the tables
of the crowned and served of Asgard.

I tangle you sweetly across the milks and
creams of my fleshy breasts.
My abdomen quivers as you lull beneath me.

Within the sweat and tremble of your arms, chest and groin,
I suckle upon you as the fullest flavors of mead deepen
within us.

Eagerly, I feel the wedge of you swell in
the carve of my tender cove.

Alone in the RIver

Well in the shapes, angles and posture of the
nudity of her evening threading
And pause, she waded softly into the fullness
of the river and felt the strokes
Of every spread of slippery weeds as they
suckled the ankles and calves
Which soothed into the dance of the nights trembling waves.

The sloping rocks of the sweeping river's edge,
I stood into the breath of southern skyline
and watched the western
Tangle of the peach hues and the drip of the sun.

I respond in curls and presses of each bead of heavy water.
I rest upon the curves of her waist and the lulling grasp
Of the clavicles and neck and the motions of her breasts.

I proclaim with shouts of the rapids, my
pressure concaves to the slouch
Of my grip against the thin stream of trickling moisture.

Sour Earth

The field grass rests stranded and heat coaxed the color yellow
and the hard brown clays of the earth.

Stepping slowly, I crossed the crimping and crunching blades
which edged beneath the blistering slap of the sun which tossed
steam upon the dried creek of the sulking valley.

Upon reaching the empty forest, I peered,
looked my way through the dead
grave of once ancient life.

Here, I stand among an endless museum of fossils,
desiring a dash upon the listles leaves,
fumbling in the slowest of winds.

I move beyond the this stretch of forgotten
maples as each nip of sap
lay dry.

I pass the tundra of these pines which
burrow in needles as they gather
gently upon the sour ground.

In the grasp of a tossing second, I breath
the aromas of the lavender bush
which boosts me in silent craving for the

once fullness of you as every
pale blush of your flesh loosens from the waters edge.
Lost in the Gleam of Morning

I starve at the touch of the fullness of you lips,
chilled as you touch me with ices and trembling cove.

I shook with the dressing fleece, gown which curled and lay
upon the shadow of the darkened room,

Flickering candles swept and throttled to every corner
and slick the feel of the calmness of her hands,
spread across me as I blinked
with waxes which sulked through the wedge of night.

Well into the madness of morning gleam,
I sauntered through the remainder of the quilt and burlap
thrown asunder.

I walk the sweet flavors of the garden as the dancing petals
marked her weave through the tiger lillies and hyacinths
carving the sweet burn of the groin of the earth.

Creek

I stood upon the shadow of dusk as the fiber of the field of rye
sweat and dampened each stalk with trembling dew beads.

Walking the edge which thrived by the
pursuance of the coolest creek,
the moonlight grazed with every row and steady stretch.

I touched her in darkness and reached to
her with the loss of her garments,
alive in the mouth of early Autumn, I quivered at the press

of the motioning grain.
with speed, the roaming pasture which hosted her softy,
the flicker of her hair and the dance of her full nakedness
struck the bloods into the deep of the nestling woods
which pressed well beyond the juices of the creek.

Wealth of the Mountain Peak

The treasury of the soil of the cascaded woodlands,
opened to the rain which pushed as plasmas down the crevice
of the earth; I stood well upon the mountain peak;
I waited for the descension of the fog, the shattered cloud.

I dripped in the vapors of skies dome.
I smelled the arrival of every sweet glistening
bud which motioned slowly
and stood upright in the limes and jades of each nurtured tree.

Tossing my vision across the vestibule of the perch of the bead,
I crossed the moan of the slicing wind and I tugged
my path to the groove of the sweet grains and clovers which filled
webbing trails and valleys, the charms,
savory swelling where the haze
shouts and whimpers for the heavens.

Deep of the Sea

Trickling water pushed beneath the stones by the oceans cove.
Just beyond the thickening warmth of the spread of evening,

I kneel to the mineral rocks and so swiftly I drank.
I look to the gliding sun as every dance
of the gluttonous moonlight
shadowed every tree and shrub, every dash and mumbling wind.

Here, gently on the last nightfall, I stretched
upon the glaze of sweet water;
I tremble in heavy flare as the quenching gush of the earth
collided with the ocean dance and I addressed the deep of the sea
and swiftly, I found treasures and charms in the shadow of night.

Lady of Morning

I slung my path to the breach of the shadowed darkness of night
and looked upon the strawberry growth
across the purple cloak of the horizon.

The cottons of the shirts I wore tenderly
soaked my back and chest as I
crossed the hills and witnessed the lady of morning.

From heavily rooted tree to the spine of the fumbling creek,
glazes of fog mumbled to the treasure I sought.

I fell to the sweet scents of the wildflower
and the well sprung mint.
With the mesh of the burning sun slapping across me,
I ran my fingers of the nearby fern and called her name.

Cobalt

The deepest meadows of green
blister beneath the shades of cobalt, basting
in the gush of the winds.

The coffee flickers steam upon my lips and face,
I angle to the west and rest by the might of the oakwood.

I stop in the nearest meadow; I place the cup upon my tongue
and I reason my way to the hilltops and pass sweet verbs as I go.

Along the Spiny Path

With the slouch and grip of the coolest of Autumn streams,
I walk nearest the edge and looked
upon the grazing pattern of blues and
emeralds which deepen into my sight.

Softly, the skies fractures open to a gushing quiver of rain.
Leaned upon a reaching trunk, soft bark of the birchwood,
I cupped my mouth, jaw and gathered a prism
well flickering into the tapping water.

In gentle remembrance, I touch the soil of the
earth and recall the breath of you
as the winds eagerly brush past my humble face.

I motion a leaf from the shaves of this whitest tree.
I toss a crimping leaf and watch as it threads
it's way along the spiny path.

Shatter of Day

Loosened, torn upon the tender Spring breeze,
I filled the lusty desires from within my lungs
and suckle upon the root of your breast.

I leaned and filled myself with the pastes of your creamy summit;
softly, I stood on the ridge, top of the jade
grass on top of the roaming hill.

In the vest of the earth I called to you.

I deepened and soothed with every molecule of the galaxy
which burnt deeply within as for the last,
I reflect upon the cool, icy grip of your hand and wrist.

I loosened the seed of you to the silent earth.

Follow the Driftwood

Tenderly, the stream tossed across the
rock and pulsed in swift currents
as an Autumn gathering of leaves swam across the waves.

I rested upon the slippery reach of the
stone, coated in the smoothest
grip of the mosses which soothed me
and held me above the water.

My humble sight, leaned to the west, captured me in trembling
flavors as the spread of the tangerine,
peach which welcomed the drip of the
sun and I entered this twilight
as the cove enters each league of the roaming ocean moan.

Listening to the dance of the sweep of the stream,
I stood and fastened my way to the threads of
driftwood which entered into the gulf.

I watched the thrash of the moaning grope which sauntered
and pulled the starving wood so deeply into the open mouth
of the tremble of this carving wash.

By pendulum swing, I watched the perfection of the rising sun;
I fade to the smoothest of waning sea.

As She Stood Above the Spread of the Lake

Gingerly, I ducked beneath the tree branches:
elm, maple, red maple, hickory, birchwood, willow
sycamore and the mighty evergreen which broomed upon me,
as I suckled upon the honey hive.

Reaching the great wash of the great lake,
I trembled and shook as the passages of the sweetest mint
call to me in tastes of the richest spots of the earth.

Pledging to the precise second of the trembling breeze
which called for me in the quivering glimpse of the heavy moon,
I removed every cloth and swam into the endless motions
of the suckling defeat as I rest with the
sanctuary of the lakes deep.

With a brooming sweep across the bounty of the hills,
I heard her call me and tug the moonlight
as she stood above the water's spread suckled
me into the swell of her breasts.

Inches Beyond

Looking across the empty fields, inches beyond Winter,
I smile to the crisp, cool breath of the early Spring,
I sling my eyes across the soil and search for the first birth of bud
and the growth of the starved, hungry field of wheat.

From the tallest of the scattering of trees,
crows land upon the eastern
edge of the great sparse field.

I turn and face the distant empty spread
of the vast grooming woodlands.

So near, the dance of the sapling thrust
and probed from the earth,
I ducked and weaved as the lime swelling pouches
furthers to the pastures, past the ancient forest.

A single crow lulls on the top of the highest pine.
Here, I pursue the flickering jams of this placid morning light
as the humble show of March softens every stretch of land.

Gardener

I touched the fullness of your cream filled breasts as the evening
danced upon the buckling rim of the rattle of the window,
edged with chips of tender white.

I swam across you and felt the pulse of
your warm, blood filled body.
I deepened my fingers across the wedge of your tangled wheat
and glazed the pale, white, flesh of your tender, eager thighs.

I tasted the fill of your fragrance which bloomed from your hair.

I looked to the eastern wall and smelled the candle
as soft wavering light shook across the room.

By the end of the rising sun,
I spoke to the quiver of her warm, blushing ears and the room
hosted the end of the dripping of wax,
I trembled into my clothes and sank upon
the sweet vapors of the garden glen.

Yellow Pollens

The thick bud swelled and popped leaving a powdery trace
of yellow pollens which spread and caked upon the coarse
crust of the earth, waiting for trembling rain.

Across the path, I ducked and walked swiftly around the shrubs
which angled the ridge and path into the woods.

I dredged my way across the wooded paths of the wooden earth.
the boast of the rising sun flickered through every tree leaf
as the moans of the nest of willow trees tossed
me in shades and groomed each
wildflower upon my breath and polished the step of my boots.

Into the absent hour of the near fading sun,
I slept by the motion of the trickling
creek and listened to the choir
of the crickets and gently
the cool soft winds dashed along my stretch and curves.

Mountain Rain

The surrounding grass reach cleverly to the midst of the trunk
as the curled, cupping leaves boasted of their veins and reached
for the approaching rains.

After an hour and a moment passed,
the solid stretch of the earth fell in the muds
as washed in the basin of the forest floor.

The moss quivered with each pat of the sliding rain.

Well into morning,
I reached the flood of the swift dashing mountain stream.
quietly,
the sparse reach of the neighboring rains sweeten upon me
as the resting fractured branches lay near the steps of my feet.

At the peak of morning, I dressed as
the vapor of the warming sun
cloaked me in the softest cottons, worn
as the baste of the hottest flesh.

Dionysus

I walked through the vineyard and stole glances upon the sweet
bloods of the earth which soothed their moisture upon
the fragrance of the tender sky.

The walking path trimmed through the middle of the tender
field and posed with rooted, soft moisture enticing the moans
of the cakes of the earth.

I feel the goblet upon the holstered cup of my gentle hands.
the sky thickens as the swell of the grape fills before me.

Fertile Earth

Gently, I lay on the full cotton blanket on the downward
slope of the emerald majestic hills as we rest and watched
the slip of the sweet azur hued stream.

Her slender arm traced and softened across my arm
as the cool Summer wind blushed across the fullness of my hair.

My rattled head rest upon the softness of her sweet breasts.
I paused, placed my mouth upon her shadowed neck
and I filled myself with the moisture of the richness
of the fluid earth.

Smoke and the Descent

The stream swept and held perfect posture as the fog fell
and spread, hung as smoke of the skies descent.

To the south, acres of pasture and stiff moistened grass
crimped beneath the soles of my leather boots.

I leaned my sight to the left and watched the rhythmic waves
of the stretching fields hug with each grasp of the ghosts
which trembled, then fade in shine of the morning sun.

I toss a pebble to the throated sounds of the sweet fluid creek.
with the sunshine pressed at my back and tender neck.

Witnessed

Alone in the blizzard skies,
The goose trembled, like a dart, through
the blustery winds and fastened
Upon an upward breeze.

Closing my eyes, I witnessed the warmth of the south
Which clung in sweet
vapors and carved to the green glades and the softest fog;
I leaned upon the white dredged fence and lended my ears
To the quivering 'caw'
as the threads of the sky lulled me to the woods where I softened
Upon the snapping fire, the edges of my face
Trickled in sweats as the snowpile melted fast.

Emerald Glaze

On the first instance of Spring, I crept through the silent forest
And hunted for the emerald glaze on the perfect clover.

I swept upon the streams edge and smelled the burning wood;
Softly I placed before the chanting crackle of the fire.

I leaned upon her and held the flesh of her torso as I
Cupped into the warmth of her mouth and rested upon her neck.

I felt the sap of the cold air drip across me as I sipped the coffee
And felt the full, scented threads upon my thigh and groin.

Into morning, I chiseled my way past
the ices and frost of the earth.
Within several moments, I lost my way and came to the clifftop
Which grooved upon the endless spread of the ocean waters.

The long stretch of the dirt path tore through the countryside
I gathered a few leaves and hurried along.

Seasonings

I walk along the quivering sands of the foams,
perching in dampness and hosting each slither of brine
which soothed across the golden stretch and golden hues.

I reach my sight to the blues melding with whites as sweet
breath of the sky trembled across me in seasoned sauce.

She left the swab of the oceans juice;
I embraced her with the slippery wash which sled her soft breasts
across me in tremors which crept within
the fastening grip of my bloods.

I trembled to the grains which sloped from the curve
of her gripping legs and the softness of her
pouch sulking within every nook.

Turning, we walked to the western lull of the spread
where western fields gathered to us in groping scents,
both fragrance and the musk which fell from the sky.

With Vapors

With vision of the blackbird,
I watched the sink of the sweeping fog
layer across the forest which hung
across the phantoms of the vapors which
clung to shrub and thicket and bush.

I felt the passions of the grooming sky at end of day.
I spoke to her with tremble and pitch
swarming across my generous throat.

I looked upon her as she faded across me, sweetly in moisture
of the tender swab where the branches and twigs sulked
the fracture of this emotive dance well across me.

In the approach of the spread of cottons,
I breathed the press and gesture which
sauntered so sweetly upon me.

I raise my head to the tender winds and open breath.
I twitch and coil upon you as the sweet and
tender touch of the ghost of you
dampened me in rippling sweats and thickening bloods.

Alone for the Night

The bedroom door spoke to me of the trembling gust
which deepened and hung across the outer hall and cautioned
a glimpse of the bed which fastened to my
patient flesh and quietly, I sobbed to the emptiness of this well
carved room, full of her dust and so distant.

Well, beneath the burlap blanket which sank upon my legs and
the mesh of my burning thigh,
I angled to the creak of the door which sobbed the vanishing
drift as I sweat to the oceans of salted rhythms, burning
across my chest and the marrow of my bones.

Now, by the deepest hour of night,
I fastened across you as you breathed across the hot gleam
of the sweat of my groin.

You return in the virgin hour of daylight and softly,
I wear the christening fracture of of the
gash which swallows every
dash of the swelling grip where I loosen to
the thick creams of her breasts.

Early Autumn and the Burgundy Leaves

I spread this swift walk across the thornbush and heavy thicket
where the snapping
buds and snapping pods freshen the forest
floor in pollens as the silent
stillness of the trees and their branches
loosen their path upon the scattering
of burgundy leaves as they shed from the red maple.

With every tamp and step upon the blood red leaves,
I pause and rest to the fall of the log which rots and melds
to the mineral rich moisture and gleam of the earth.

I feel the sweat slither across my heavy face
as I trembled to the gashing
press of the Autumn winds.

I deepen my theshing thirst as the pond
and nearby slicing stream
gegs and feeds before me.

I Slumber Near the Twisting Vines

Vines of the moan of the trembling trees of the forest
stood silent and held the vines as they wrapped sweetly
across bend, branch and trunk.

I ducked beneath the clamor of the shadow of the sweetened
mint which spread softly across the minerals in each path.

I filled my lungs with the roaming
flavors which shook from edge of the
woods to the edge of the woods.

Evening wrangled and fell to the shadow of night.
winds rattled across the treetops and gently sang in tender
crackling of the moon shining across the snap of the fire.

Whispering to the glaze of the humble winds,
I softened in a mesh of the trickling forest waters
as they sauntered to the mask of the earth.

Near the crisp carriages of morning, I fell
gently to a slumber and wavered
across the spirit of the sauces of shower and host
of the ember of the wood.

Dreams Before Daylight

The pond tossed flavors of kelp and film
gently, I knelt to the murky green and
loosened to a softening sleep.

With the ambrosia of the tender grip
of her as her soft, warm hands
burrowed through my denim and pulled upon the wedge of me,

I slandered the howl of the winds and turned to the paleness
of her breasts as I shook into the carving stretch of night.

Awakening to the crimp and flash of daylight,
I reach the peak of the caverns which drip before me.

Into the soft fields where the pine needles
spread across the woodland floor,
the lull of the tender light floundered to the bend of her

As I gripped each pattern of her blouse
which grooved upon the forest floor.

Answering With the Rain

The staff prodded into the soft mesh and moss which
nursed the growth of the earth.

I stepped to the broadened trail and sulked beneath the piercing
howls of the ginger, lavish wind.

I wrangled and swept beneath the wools of my coat
as dewdrops rest upon the lime green
buds I passed along the way,
so deeply traveled into the woodlands.

WIth the beginning of the patter of the rain,
I drank from the cupping curve of the leaf
and drew sap with the maple

and sap from the pine.

Searching For Her Nudity

In the nudity of the Summer glades and the passing stream,
I removed every stitch and deepened
into the gushing gash of water.

Across my genitals and the edged genitals
lumbering near the sweeping water,
I looked for her in all perfect nakedness.

I strode knee deep and found the pebbles and edged rocks which
burrowed beneath the curve of my foot.

I spoke to you with the passing wind as
the rumbling pastures spoke
of the soft, deepest green of every field and meadow.

You fade into the wavering cove and deepened
into me with the pale, fibers of your
flesh and the black stones of your tender eyes.

Bakery

I spoke as the baker of your perfect dough breasts.
Lively, the powders of the sheer shadowed angles and curves,
I looked and shook to the tremble of every finish.

I relish with you upon the carpet of the floor
settled upon the stove, I swept my hands against my genitals,
alone in the hearth of this solitary dwelling.

The settlement of the moist cove of your mouth
wrestled upon the sweet fibers, from fireplace to the lean
of the grooming locks of hair which trellised across me
well into the shadows of the fade of you,
each icy finger cultivated me in crepes and the bread
which I lean upon and fasten to my tooth.

Crystal Blue

I stood and watched the flood of the basin
and gorge of the river's edge.
Quietly, the sun tamped upon the brown
murk of the deep of the water
and I stood closely and listened to the whimper of the clover
and I felt the mush of the mosses and joy of the dancing ferns.

The stretching trees relished as I deepened into the woods
and felt the small, slender tributaries pour fresh lulls of the fruit
which scattered in the raspberry bush and patch of strawberry
reaching for the morning sun, climbing to the east.

I combed the rapture and pleasure of the
earth spreading upon the quaking
smash of the sunshine, an eager light in the baste
of the dashing Summer sun.

Gone. I felt the pressure of the winds
across the broadness of my back.
I travelled to the east and suckled the found blue crystal water
which drew me in small rivets.

I answer you in prisms of the sky.

Looking for Pastures

The sky floods in gnarled gray and ivory white,
I stand under the marbled dome as the sting of swift
rain suckles the cloth I wear, heavy paste.

Walking across the fattened field of sweet lime green, I
feel the sobbing heel and sole of the deepened boots,
I flood my way in the swiveling stream
as I relish in the nakedness and fresh dance.

Clear warmth of the shattered sky,
I toss myself to the pebbled road and further my way with
cascading leaves of the perfect green.

Upon the nearest sloping hill,
I tread to the trembling waver of the forest
branches and the forest leaves.

I answer the invitation of the pasture ahead and softly I sleep
in the dry, crisp, emerald, shattered grass.

Wash

I stand near the glint and glimmering pond
And I stand by the sliver of a breeze as the look of me
Shatters to the distortion of my painted green murk which
Soaks within every reflection of the heaviest woods.

I kneel and trace my finger upon the trembling wash.

Swiftly, I deepen into the endlessness of the
grooming, lust of the woodlands,
Alive and so visceral to the orange and peach painted sky,
Alive in the heaviest hour of evening.

Searching in the Moment of Morning

The rain slept upon the floor of the woods and I
stepped upon the porridges of the earth and faced to the east
and hustled across the shaking wildflowers of the meadow
as sweet aromas filled me.

Pausing, I harnessed the warmer winds as they stroked the beard
and leather skin of my sun soaked face.

By morning, the dance of the flicker of early light
seasoned me in the thin path I covet as each step
led me to the rolling surface upon the higher ground.

The sweet call of the mourning dove
sauntered to the grip of my ears.
I leaned upon the hickory tree as the blitz of the earliest
sounds flood across the strain of the tall sprout of the field.

Crows Fly Through the Slapping Rain

Early Spring blended into Autumn as I walked with scattered
tracks across of the sweet moisture of this country road.

This maple boasted of the fangs of these leaves
which sank as a soft gathering along the stretching, open field.

Looking above, I watched the crows
pepper the egg blue sky, then
gather to the canvas and treetops as the softest rain tapped upon
every reach of every branch, quivering to the hot sun
as the slap of the rain soothed the clay of the earth into muds.

I looked upon you as the arms spread
and towered across the basin
of the trunk where the sauces arranged in file and suite.

Great Oak

These woods spoke of their antiquity and
spoke of the curving vine,
the oldest marrow soaked within the oldest soil, moaning
with the scurry of the quickness of the breathing winds which
tremble across the loosest soil, coolness
within the scatter of these trees.

Finding the cakes of these tender mosses,
I rested with the angle of my face upon the moisture
where these minerals dust across with the approach of the wind.

Deepened upon the hillside the great oak stood silent and spoke
of the ancient moments when she rested alone on the heavy hill.

With the caress of the blooming shadow of the blackest night,
leaves scatter as a silhouette.

My Closure of Day

I sweetly walk across the soft meadow of the warm breeze, I thirst
as the puddling creek spools across my feet and I kneel and drink.

Into the absence of the once white gown of
the sky which grazed and thinned
across the flickering fog upon the surface of each grass spear,

I placed my finger across the cupping drop of threaded dew,
I place the droplet upon the tip of my
yearning tongue and sweetly

The soak and thickness of the sky swelled
within the edge of my mouth.

Walking the edge of the brook, I stumble
and reach the basin of the Mountain
which hosted each rise of the tender path.
I fade upon the rest as the peak of the
mountain height, I loosen to the
threads of the downward slope.

Touch of Rain

I spoke to you of caverns of the smoothness of your thighs
and small, pooling, trickling streams which cooled from
the quiver and trickle from the shadows of your breasts.

Nearing the edge of morning, I lay the warmth of my face
upon the soft heat of your abdomen and shook you in the laces
which slither and crawl across the sweet
flavors of your torso and flesh.

The sky swelled and gushed upon us in heavy, pouring rain
as the cloth we wore suckle to the pastes of our skin.

Into the depth of the morning flash,
alive in the pinks, peaches, and amber hues,
I drew you near to me and coveted each
of your inches of lusty breads.

Phantoms in the Morning Hours

Mist fell like phantoms across the grassy earth,
scattered with piles of the sweet breath of morning.

Small webs of the grooming dance of clover
spread across the narrow path as soft wind hosted as a treasure

A gem which flooded the early sky with angles and tender verbs,
an announcement of layering fog.

lean along the chipped white fence which practised upon me
in measure and thick grooming from the pockets of the open sky.

With a keen vision, I watched her
fade to the triumph of the quest for morning.

Evening Chill

Listening to stones scurrying across the deep lunge of the cliff,
I feel the breath from the sky swipe across the drip of my face
and softly I return to the path, leading
to the emeralds of the valley
which held me upon a groove which dashes me in powders
and weakens the concave spread of my
head and trembling shoulders.

Along the route, path, you hold me in every rhythm as the sweet
warm sun dashes across me.

This pasture which coddles me suspends me in relics of this most
ancient hills as they speak of nocturnes which
lull me in the heaviest hour of night.

I slept in the arms of the majestic and quivered to the soothing
grip of the evening chill.

Garden and Grotto

Sweet motions of the garden and grotto, the swiveling and dance
of the onion grass floundered upon the wind.

I breath each layer
of fragrance and aroma as they lay upon the stretch of grass;
gently, I fill my lungs and tremble to the most distant hills
which arrive and I blossoms to threads of the shattered petals.

The bust of her, shaped as a flood of
open streams pouring creams,
I gathered her and shook warmth upon
her as the descension of the sky
crowned you in laurels and tapered you in fig leafs.

I felt your breath against the burn of my perched, waiting ears.

I grasp you into the grip of my arms and writhe within you
as the patterns of your lace lay as a map of every open road.

Storm Passes

I reach the eastern ridge of the park and slowly
the morning flecks of the morning sun
cascades across my trembling sight.

I meet you by the gush of the slip of the stream and gently
I wade through the soothing pebbles and smile upon you
as you warmly embrace me and touch the
curve of my hips and sweetly pass
the groin and thigh which rivets through me.

Looking upward, I watch the approaching
threads of the eager storm.

I touch the neck you expose and I feel
the sting of you perfect nails.

In the passing smash of the rain, I deepen
through you and saunter
into the neighboring woods and I slumber
with you on the softness
of the grouping, gathering of needles fallen from the pine.

I awake in the mists of the presence of daylight.
I stand in the sober sun and walk my way so far to the north.

As I Fade You Dance Nude Upon the Pebbled Shore

I strode across the jousting weeds, thorns
and wrapping vines of the earth.
Sweetly, I lifted and grappled the lofting scent of the mint
which carried across the fattened growth of the meadow.

Beneath the rhymes of the rattling
branches which slung to the cove
where I settled and listened to the choir of the oceans and all
temptations of the fugue.

Although you were present, I sulked and
looked upon you as the nakedness
of you edged across pebbles and swimming kelp which tangled
across the brooming ocean sand.

Farthest to the west, I returned and sank
into the rich velvets of the earth.
I recall you as I deepen into the wealth of the soil which calls
to me and wrestles me in dances of the trellising flesh.

Asleep During Daytime

The rain smacked the floor of the crimping burn of the field
as the steam drifted to the pasture and grazed to the thickest
of woods which settled with a browned edge
of needle and chip of the cone.

A year past at this precise moment and
measure, I smiled upon the endless
shades of green as they carved their way upon the freshest
of carpeted of grass and I slung my sight upon the blackbird

which sang of the trembling heat and
lusty desire to the frequency
of the woodlands and all smothering sight.

I continued past along the watery spine of the earth.
I drank and cleared the parchment of my throat.

Alone in the fatness of these forest grooves
and champions of green
and champions of daylight, I suckled
upon the moisture of the earth
and returned to the seed of every core.

Delicate

I listened to the womb of you as tender
shades of the darkest of hours
saunter past and soothed your path to the hollow of the woods.

I listened again and softly, the sky screamed
and shook every nut and aging
leaf from branch to the fertility of the earth.

The soil lulled with roots risen and the
bedding of leaves and needles
carpeting along each tremor
of the fangs of her as she cast the wooden nut and chipped cone.

I brewed my lust and dashed across to her and sweetly
I placed my lips and tongue upon the
perfection of her full breaded breasts.

The waver of the branch trickled upon me and gently I relished
in her quiet flesh; eagerly the burgundy of her flesh

Lingered to my burning chest and my burning genitals as she
placed her delicate hands upon me.

Past the Ocean Pearl

Through the descension of the falling clouds
which thickened upon the grasses
cupping beads of dew, a tremble of the
ocean pearl, I knelt, then lay upon
the shoots and spread of the fallen leaf.

Quietly, I soften beneath the gluttony of the swelling moon.
as a pasture of the falling quilt of the sky,
I pause and then coat myself to the chill
of the empty mountaintop.

I speak to the pregnancy of the buried seeds
as the moisture sweeps across me and the shavings, fog and haze,
sweetens in the ordination of the quiet sovereignty.

I stand, gather and walk the field as the silent fog
suckles upon the sky and gently I walk to the forest and nook
which thrusts every fertile pollen into the
drift of the woodland swell.

Upon reaching the edge of the woods,

I carve my way to the buried seed.

Spring Rain

I tremble my way through the threads of the forest weeds.
Quick, I tangle my way across the thorns and thicket
which slowly open to the glaze of the glades which open as
a fabric and hem of the stitches burrowing
through the emerald glen.

In the dash of a moment past, the
tapping rain soothed across me
and I soaked in the wash of this slivered sky.

The sweetness of this paternal canvas where the cloak of the sky
patterned in hues of gray and the fade of the pale white.
reaching the slithering bend of the forest creek,
I walked and dipped through the pasture and
entered the baste of the gushing water.

I lean across the trunk of the heavy width of the towering tree.
sweet rain filled my lungs with the most delicate of senses.

Starvation

I remained alive in the moment where the flaxen hued grass
spoke of the soft patter of rain which
returns in the caress of April.

Cobalt blue lightning quivered and tangled with the oaks spread
sweetly upon the field.

Dressed in cottons and denim, the suckling fasten of the rain,
the chill of the tender garments, soothed me to a calm chill.

Chymes of the walk deepened my boots upon the moistest mud.

Well into the chill of this starving nightfall, I
walked through the patterns
of the dancing sky as each probe of weather sweetened the death
of the fields of yellow grass.

Across the field, I sauntered and walked
through the robes of the Spring
fixture where the gap and puddles drenched every post and slight
of the roaming creek.

Blue Velveteen

I smile upon the fresh draft of the soothing night.
Mountain winds cascade upon me as the tremble of the mist
presses so sweetly upon my torso, hair and bust.

I travel into the carving howl and scream
of the burrowing woods
where the slumbering hollow of the woods threads through
blue velveteen of the fall of the tender sky.

I speak of this as you flood past the garden fence,
pond and sweetened climb of the ivy and vines.

I encounter you as you tenderly thrust
through the baste of the meadow,
soft red climb of the reach of the barn.

Soft, I touch you upon the girth of your arms and the softness
of your pulsing, throbbing thighs, the saunter of your breasts.

The sky opened to the white pitch of
morning as the bedding where
you lay speaks of your absence.

Dance of Night

The fibers carrying scents traveled sweetly
across this stretch of woods.
Shuffling the edge of my feet, the leaves
breathed to the falling clouds
of the crow peppered sky.

Drinking my way upon the roaming floods of the creek,
I suckled mt boots well into the earth and youthfully
I watched the distant playfulness of the
bluebird as the distant chapel
sulked between us in pathways of cobblestone and cedar chips
which gathered by shrub and bush.

Tenderly, I spoke to the thud of each tolling bell.
Into the magnitude of the trembling grasses
which soured in limes across
the sweet tender hills,
I leaned upon the shadow of the lines of the trees;
quietly, I leaned upon the trunk of the birchwood
and slept into the dance of night.

With the Cherry Blossom

Standing so near the tremble of the white cherry blossom,
I collected the leaves of the petals and
placed them upon the cushions
sulking smoothly upon the bed and tapered quilt.

I stretch my legs and roam the pastures and fields
as each wildflower and fullness of every tree
loosened the shedding leaves as silent winds coated and shook.

I loosened myself by the warm pond
waters and sank each foot deeply.
I drank the patter of the falling winds
which softened each posture
of the angled reach of my face and bust.

I felt the touch of the icy trembling hands
as they quivered to the wind.
softly the sky scurried every drop of moisture and the cherry tree
writhed upon me as the branches slapped
and melded with moans,
tender upon the widening path.

From the Hickory Tree

I suckle upon the milk of the infancy of life.
The rains spool and drizzle off the stretch of the eaves
as the warm breath off the southern gale
lurks and lives within me;
I tremble to the most distant gush of
syrups pooling across my tongue.

I pause and shake at the quiver of the hickory tree
which washes each leaf on each branch
and fondles the grassy mounds.

I shake loose the droplets of the water bead;
I look upon the deep of the east and I lust
to the moss and saps of each tree
as I walk slowly and thread my way upon the dense
tremor of the soak of the forest.

I recall the breasts of her and the syrup of life.
I quiver to the lush of the shattered wood
which fell from blitzes of lightning
and the mesh upon the quivering ground.

By the end of each day, I smelled the lush
squelch of the starlit woods.

Searching

I dashed from maize to barley to open stretch of field.
Puddles lulled and lusted to the ponds stitches and cloth
which triumph the tenderness of the dancing
squelch where kelp and sod gave proclamation
of aftermath and residue.

I pronounced a path as the quivering
shadows of the flooding grope
Of the deepest pasture of nightfall harbored within me.

I soothed my way across open plains and
soaked the warmth of the midday sun.

On a specific settling evening where the clouds of night
Saddles the probe of the your looseness,

I sauntered the breath of you
as the stitches of your cloth fell to the saddle of the ground.

I pressed my lips against the warmth of your flesh and sweetly
The sting of your eyes threw darts and arrows upon my fiery skin.

Waiting Until Morning

Deep night,
I sling my sight to the carve and drip of the nectar of the ivory
colored candle as the wax speaks so silent, I listen with
the lean of my eyes.

This wax trembles across me in tears of
the flickering dance of night.

I disrobe as the floods of her which saunter across the nightfall
and the sting of the night's gem.

I slept upon her into the breads of perching
milk which swell and fill
the baskets of her breasts.

By morning, I tenderly found my way.

Night's Assembly

I walk the hallways of the deepest stretch of the forest.
The moon angles and fumbles across me
in the tremor of a silent wash
as the mulch and cedar chips patterned to the steps of my feet.

The hyacinth blossomed and danced upon
the moisture of the threaded
floor of the richness of the woods.

I coarsed my fingers through the fine
silks of her full blooming hair.
I witnessed the most pale of breasts as
they sauntered before my lips.

Here, the sweet voice which rose in assembly above the earth;
I tangle with you as each flood
of the rain at night dampened you and dampened me.

The fine groove and patch of moss fondled me in the dark lunacy
of each dash of the black skies of harvesting night.

Last Breath

The grass grew to my calves as the mint
scattered and stewed perfect scents
deeply and full within the edges of my lungs.

Stood upon the slight rise of the hill,
I glanced enamored and watched the
moon rise through the branches
and along the stretch of the trunk.

I slept beneath the falling leaves and
curled and slept into the farthest
depth of the cloth of the night's sky.

I awoke, tucked sweetly in the rich soils of the earth.
every toss of mineral and seed
coiled across me and I moaned with the howl of the slicing wind.

Now, Spring.
I fed my way to the silent birth of the
stewing seed and the rising grass.

You walk across me and I quiver in the dampness of each joust
of the shoot, weed and spread.

Past Blue Creek

The blue creek tumbled and drained
through the heavy tufts of speared
grass as the earliest of morning moments polished dewdrops
upon the shavings and pointed spread of the onion grass;
I spoke to the nurtured field and wept to
the sting of the roaming spices
which trembled under the soles of my boots
and snipped my open calves.

I halted at the caress of the brook and drank the life from it
as each rocky smooth touch motioned and mumbled to me;
quietly, I suckled the mist, dripping upon my flesh and tenderly
the sky opened and soothed upon me.

Between here and the rise and joust of the reaching mountain
I motioned to the gray slicing wind.

With the age of each portion of the day, I
slumbered to the bloom of the glen.
The cloth I wear shows perfect presentation of the moaning rains.
The sky grooved as a highway which swept across me and sweetly
I loosened upon the brittle trail.

Seeds in the Dark Hour

I fell upon the tender moisture and heavy aroma of the soil
which brought the dusts of my ancestors
to the grotto, garden and field.

I felt the warm Summer winds and they trembled across my face
and mangled to the dampness of each reach and floating pollen,
caressing the wet muds and roots of every maple.

I stood silent and watched the sun sink in the west
as hues of the sky, nectarines and apricots,
dredged and dampened beneath my feet, across
my torso and across my leathery face.

I shook and released every seed of every bud as the width
of me warmed the fabrics I wore and tenderly;
I polished and groomed the softest soils
which threaded me to the voices
blooming across the tender field.

A few hours later, I fell upon the dampness
and faded to the gown of scarlet
which tackled upon me in the deep of the touch of night.

Beneath the Pines and With the Rains

I felt the threads of this cotton shirt and vest.
I spoke to the land and the leaves loosened
and gathered upon me.
The damp dome of the tender blue sky
tossed the winds and hosted
the burning stretch of the hustling sun.

With clothing removed, I walked to the pond which lay so still
and offered me the kelp and film which sauntered relentless.

Listening to the dash of the sky and the opening of every cloud,
I drank the beads of rain as the moaning pond held a drizzle,
crooned to me in all temporal laughter.

I found her by the nearby pond and
holding the cupping smallness
of her hands, I wedged into the pond and looked to the sky
as I burned in fluids and bloods.

Together we touched and trembled
through milks and ivory creams.

Voices of the Woods

I listened to the banter of the willow tree, much as I
listened to the elm tree and the oak.

Each branch dusted the grass and brown
and tan patches of the earth.
With muscle of the age and the spirit of the wood,
I witnessed and heard every tree speak of the spirits they
hide and caress within the ancient branches which covet the
spirits and nymphs as the glaze of Autumn relishes
a trembling dance.

Listening further, I heard the croon and
creak of each splinter of wood.
Now,
the leaves stripped in emptiness,
caresses as the sky waltzed before the shade of night.

Dust and Dirt

Winds wrestle the dust and dirt off the slender country road.

The dome of the sky moaned to a deepend scream as I
quivered beneath this swiftness, I met sweetly the rain
which fumbled to the earth and lovingly fastened puddles
upon the rocks and rivets.

The sky gave birth to tendrils and sweeping gales as the fragrances
dampened and shuttered with each breeze.

Reaching the base which led to the peak of the mountain,
alive with powdery glaze, in a toss of moments, I
reach the pinnacle and felt the bloods of this heavy nature.

I freed myself of these clothes, wools and cottons and denim.
I calmly looked upon the dusty earth and
watched the limes blossom to emeralds
and the smallest of creeks fasten into a flex of stream,
tied to the dashing river.

Country Nudity

She opened, removed her clothing for me and slithered forth
as the tide of the slowest country river, I suspend my walk
past the groove of this feathered plot of
grass, hosting the blackbirds
which suckled each dewdrop in tenderness and passions.

I softly placed my palms upon her goblets and I leaned
forward and drank every cream.

Lust bloomed through this Spring thresh of sweeping air.
I caressed you as the deep of the forest spoke to us and soothed
my arrangement upon the needles of the pinewood floor.

You found me in passages of leagues after leagues
spread quickly along the drift of the woodland floor.

Smoke and Fog

With dust and ash, I loafe upon the wind and fastened
to the mountaintop, only to loosen across the zenith and gently
land in the glades of greens and bark
and trunks of tan and brown.

I lull into the fragrance of the earth.
the smoke and fog of the mountain
range settled and spoke of me
as I entered each lung and smoothed across
each chest, abdomen and breast.

On the next moment, I swam the width of the straining river,
I trembled and danced to the fertility of the moss and quiver
of the fern which sought after ankles and calves, deep within
the showered grass which tamped and
depressed calmly and tenderly.

In the morning, I vanished to the warmth of the rising fog.

Seeds and the Youthful Spring

I toss seeds upon the clay and dirt which spreads across this
dead country field.

I feel my feet carve upon the vast aged country trail
as every dying womb of the earth retreats to the sweetest
gathering where a single leaf of the sycamore
curls, cups and cradles the seed
blowing wildly across the sky.

I advance to the mountainside and calmly
I sweeten my face and glaze
as the fumbling twigs and branches lull
across the trickling juice of the
youthful spring.

I drink deeply and saute my path to the snows of the north.

In the Park

Sitting gently in the shaved green grass of the park,
I absorb every gushing wind which threads upon the fullness
of my hair and dances upon my eager flesh.

The apple tree sheds dozens of apples as the
sweet fumes from breeze to breath
fumble upon the earth and speak of a shallow grave.

I walk aside the swiftest of creeks as the moisture of the water
cascades and cools me in tenderness and icy sweat.

I feel the earth soft beneath me as the rain
peppered the ground in moments.
I lit a smoke and walked the well groomed path.

The Three Fates

The hair grew and unfolded to the supple
grip and stretch of the finger.

High in the tower top, the three ladies
perched upon the velvet chairs
With hair hung as a drape.

Perfect glisten of this flaxen colored hue spread an endless lock
and she smiled upon the distant screams of each muscling voice.

The hands, delicate and supple, coaxed every
strand and fastened every lock.

The oldest of ladies held these sheaves in the grip of madness.

I soaked my way across the river and shook
at the sweet voice of the three fates.

At the Stream

His hands were pale, sculpted as ivory as each
muscle within his arms, chest and shoulders lurked beyond me,
alive in the moisture of the calmest of streams.

I removed my shoes and lifted the legs of my denim.

I sweetened my way across the fumbling
rapids and stepped upon
every rock and pebble, every reach of kelp
and across the tender films
which threshed across the water.

I look above and watch the justice moon crave every
droplet of moisture from the spread of my chest and bust.

I look upon him, my friend and I direct to the pathway
which led us to the crest and eave of my home.

Ocean Waves

The ocean cried out as a choir and the brine soothed and dances
across the grains of sand as every tug of moisture
trembled in the quake of my shuddering mouth,
alive in the most generous sea.

As she walked naked across the dunes and basted in the dunes,
I wept to the plunge of the dome of the sky and softly
I grew sweet to the nearby hives of honey which trembled
through me and lanced upon me.

I turn and look upon the ebbing tide and in a dash
I look back and the perfect sweats of you and the perfect curve
trembled upon me and fade beneath the ocean waves.

Refuge

Green leaves tugged upon by the wind held
above me as a canvas and swept
across me in the spindling haze of a dream.

I awoke and walked past the white shavings of the birchwood
and sweetly, I trembled past each stone and fallen branch.

Winds increased and the sloping sky
burrowed in grays and colors of the ashewood.

I stood and fasten to the deeper ache of
the woodlands as once silent
vowels spoke to me of their chants and sweet choirs,
tenderly alive in the shaken avenue of this forest.

I reached the girth and breadth of the cave
as I slumbered in and sipped
the cool coffee, tangles upon my mouth
carved as the slashing trees.

Refuge

Green leaves tugged upon by the wind held
above me as a canvas and swept
across me in the spindling haze of a dream.

I awoke and walked past the white shavings of the birchwood
and sweetly, I trembled past each stone and fallen branch.

Winds increased and the sloping sky
burrowed in grays and colors of the ashewood.

I stood and fasten to the deeper ache of
the woodlands as once silent
vowels spoke to me of their chants and sweet choirs,
tenderly alive in the shaken avenue of this forest.

I reached the girth and breadth of the cave
as I slumbered in and sipped
the cool coffee, tangles upon my mouth
carved as the slashing trees.

Endless Path

I toss the seeds upon the open stretch of the garden
where the moans of the earth offer secrets and I delve swiftly
across the garden field of wildflowers and trembling leaves.

I succumb to the sample of the cool chills
of the early Spring morning
and softly I tremble to the shaking wind
which catches each part of me in the richness of the earth.

I surrender to you as you arrive early and
dampen my hands and thread
your fingers along the groove of my groin.

I face my path to the east and in sweeping strides,
I caress the rise of the sun which flickers upon me and softly
I walk the endless path through the endless path of the woods.

I lay upon the Summer earth as
I surrender to the floods of dust.

About the Author

Donny Barilla, a poet covering the realms: human intimacy, nature, mythology, theology, and man's relationship with death and the departed, has been writing for over three decades. He writes daily and strives to renew himself as an artist from page to page and body of work to body of work. Very seldom does he take a break from writing as he views it as a full-time job. He lives a reclusive lifestyle and finds himself clinging close to nature and all her elements. His home state of Pennsylvania strikes chords of poetic depth about him as he finds loveliness from cornfield to meadow. Whether it's feelings of love, intimacy, or a special closeness, he maintains the feeling that death does not take these with him/her to the grave. Emotions and feeling outlast the flesh of the human body. Human intimacy draws near an enigmatic spiritual passion which conquers all on the prismatic scale of experience. When speaking of mythology Donny says, "myths were created to make sense of feelings which are complicated by very nature. They are perhaps more easily understood through persons greater than oneself. As for theology, a disciplined aspect, incorporates quite finely with passions and secured poetic comforts.
https://twitter.com/BarillaDonny

www.ingramcontent.com/pod-product-compliance
Lightning Source LLC
Chambersburg PA
CBHW032228080426
42735CB00008B/766